# japanese

GW00385067

# japanese

## DELICATE AND SUBTLE DISHES
## FROM AN ELEGANT CUISINE

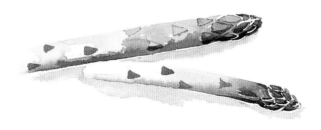

masaki ko

**southwater**

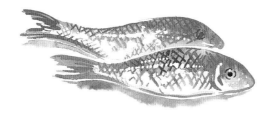

This edition is published by Southwater

Southwater is an imprint of Anness Publishing Ltd
Hermes House, 88–89 Blackfriars Road, London SE1 8HA
tel. 020 7401 2077; fax 020 7633 9499
www.southwaterbooks.com; info@anness.com

© Anness Publishing Ltd 1997, 2004

UK agent: The Manning Partnership Ltd, 6 The Old Dairy, Melcombe Road, Bath BA2 3LR; tel. 01225 478444; fax 01225
478440; sales@manning-partnership.co.uk
UK distributor: Grantham Book Services Ltd, Isaac Newton Way, Alma Park Industrial Estate, Grantham, Lincs NG31 9SD; tel.
01476 541080; fax 01476 541061; orders@gbs.tbs-ltd.co.uk
North American agent/distributor: National Book Network, 4501 Forbes Boulevard, Suite 200, Lanham, MD 20706; tel. 301 459
3366; fax 301 429 5746; www.nbnbooks.com
Australian agent/distributor: Pan Macmillan Australia, Level 18, St Martins Tower, 31 Market St, Sydney, NSW 2000; tel. 1300
135 113; fax 1300 135 103; customer.service@macmillan.com.au
New Zealand agent/distributor: David Bateman Ltd, 30 Tarndale Grove, Off Bush Road, Albany, Auckland; tel. (09) 415 7664;
fax (09) 415 8892

All rights reserved. No part of this publication may be reproduced, stored in a retrieval system, or transmitted in any way or by
any means, electronic, mechanical, photocopying, recording or otherwise, without the prior written
permission of the copyright holder.

A CIP catalogue record for this book is available from the British Library.

Publisher  Joanna Lorenz
Senior Cookery Editor  Linda Fraser
Project Editor  Zoe Antoniou
Designer  Ian Sandom
Illustrations  Madeleine David
Photography  Juliet Piddington
Styling  Marion Price
Food for photography  Carol Tennant
Cover: Photography  Nicki Dowey  Stylist  Emma Patmore  Design  Wilson Harvey

Previously published as part of the Classic cookery series

1 3 5 7 9 10 8 6 4 2

For all recipes, quantities are given in both metric and imperial measures, and, where appropriate, measures are also given in
standard cups and spoons. Follow one set, but not a mixture, because they are not interchangeable.

Picture on frontispiece shows (left to right): Five-flavour Noodles and Individual Noodle Casseroles

# CONTENTS

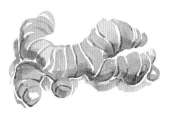

# INTRODUCTION

**J**apanese cuisine is an orchestrated symphony of art. The style of cooking is simple but simplicity is the most difficult characteristic to achieve. The Japanese cook respects individual ingredients and prepares them with care to ensure that each flavour is brought out in the dish.

Cooking methods and eating habits are very closely linked to historical circumstances in Japan. For example, a policy of meat prohibition from 1603 to 1867, in an attempt to stop aggression in the population, meant that fish became very popular. Also, the fact that Japan is an island gave the people access to a diverse range of different fresh fish, and the custom of eating the fish raw emerged.

There are many vegetables unique to Japan that are nutritious and healthy. Tofu, first introduced from China, has become immensely popular. Noodles, also introduced from China, have since become almost as widely eaten as Japanese rice.

Fresh raw ingredients are used for dishes such as the famous sushi and sashimi, where the skill is in the preparation of the food rather than literally in the cooking method. Another widely practised technique is that of grilling. As a fish-eating nation, much care is taken over perfecting this. It is very important to grill food well to ensure that it retains its

flavour and stays moist without being adversely affected by the fierce heat or by the burning charcoal. Finally, boiling in various types of stock is another classic Japanese cooking method. Boiled dishes are warming and nutritious.

The Japanese alphabet is made up of a series of consonants followed by vowels. For example, the way to express the "S" character is *sa, shi, su, se* and *so*. This also happens to relate to the seasonings used in Japan. The following list shows the exact order in which seasonings are applied to dishes, based on scientifically tested logic. The theory is that bigger particles, such as sugar, cannot penetrate foods when obstructed by smaller particles, such as salt. The following seasonings should always be used in a correct sequence as shown here.

*Sa*   stands for *sato* which is sugar, used in marinades and sauces.

*Shi*   stands for *shio* or salt.

*Su*   stands for *su*, vinegar, which should not be added too early because it evaporates when heated and loses its flavour.

*Se*   stands for *shoy* or *seyuy*, which is soy sauce, also added at the end of cooking or to flavour food before eating.

*So*   stands for miso paste that is used in many dishes.

*Next page shows (from left to right): Prawn and Egg-knot Soup and Mixed Vegetable Soup.*

# GLOSSARY

**ADUKI BEANS**   Small, red sweet beans, used in desserts, also available in glacé form (*ama-natto*) or in a paste (*neri-an*).

**BONITO**   In Japanese cooking, the Pacific bonito, a small tuna, is commonly used. It is the strongest flavoured of the tuna and is used dried, in thin flakes known as *katsuo-bushi*. It is used to flavour stock and is sprinkled over dishes to season.

**DASHI**   A stock providing the underlying flavour for most dishes.

**GOBO**   Known as *burdock*, this is a long, thin root vegetable. It may be soaked to remove bitter flavours and eaten raw, or cooked.

**HIJIKI**   This dried seaweed is soaked and used in soups and salads.

**JAPANESE SPRING ONIONS**   Known as *negi*, these are larger than the European spring onions, with longer, thicker, blue-green stems.

**KATAKURI-KO**   Potato starch or flour. Cornflour can be used instead.

**KOMBU**   Kelp seaweed that flavours stock and is served as a vegetable. Dried kombu is dark grey-brown with a pale powdery covering. It is just wiped before use.

*Picture shows a selection of Japanese seasoning ingredients typical to this cuisine (clockwise from bottom left): Miso paste, Kombu seaweed, Wasabi paste, Umeboshi and Katakuri-ko.*

**KONNYAKU**   A cake made from flour produced from a root vegetable called devil's tongue. Tear it into pieces before cooking so that it absorbs more flavour. Black and white varieties are available.

**MIRIN**   Sweet cooking sake, this has a delicate flavour and is usually added in the final stages of cooking.

**MISO**   Fermented paste of soya beans, the key ingredient for miso soup and widely used as a seasoning. There are various types, depending on the culture used to ferment them, which may be based on barley, wheat or soya bean starter mould. White miso has a lighter flavour than red miso but it is saltier. Dark brown miso is a strong-flavoured version.

**MOOLI**   Long white radish, also known as *daikon*. About the size of a parsnip (or larger), mooli has a crunchy texture and peppery flavour similar to red radishes but milder. It may be cooked or served raw in salads, grated for dips or used as a garnish.

**NARI**   Pale pink ginger pickles that are served with sushi or sashimi, to refresh the palate between bites. *See* Pickles.

**NOODLES**   Various types are used. *Soba* are long, thin buckwheat noodles often used in dishes from east Japan. *Somen* are round white wheat flour noodles. *Udon* are white ribbon noodles available fresh or dried. These are used in the cuisine of west Japan.

**NORI**   Dried seaweed, sold in paper-thin sheets which are dark green to black in colour and almost transparent in places. It is toasted and used as a wrapping for sushi. Ready-toasted sheets (*yaki-nori*), seasoned with ingredients such as soy sauce, salt and sesame oil, are also readily available from health food shops.

**PICKLES** Pickled vegetables (*tsukemono*) are often served with rice dishes. Fresh root ginger is also pickled in various strengths of flavour.

**RICE VINEGAR** A pale vinegar with a distinctive, delicate flavour that should not be confused with Chinese rice vinegar.

**SAKE** Japanese rice wine. It is not necessary to use expensive sake for cooking. Sake is drunk hot or chilled.

**SASHIMI** Slices of raw fish.

**SESAME SEEDS** Black or white, these are available roasted or plain. The plain seeds should be toasted before use.

**SEVEN FLAVOUR SPICE OR PEPPER** This chilli-based spice, known as *shichimi*, is made of hemp, poppy, rape and sesame seeds, anise-pepper leaves and tangerine peel.

**SHIITAKE MUSHROOMS** The most popular mushroom in Japan, this has a good flavour, especially when dried. Soaking water from dried shiitake makes a good stock.

**SHIRATAMA-KO** Rice flour made from glutinous short grain rice with a high starch content. This is used to make *mochi* (sticky rice cakes).

**SHISO LEAVES** A Japanese herb similar to basil.

**SOY SAUCE** There are several different types of Japanese soy sauce. Chinese soy sauce should not be substituted as it is far stronger. *Usukuchi* soy sauce is light in colour but it has a saltier taste than dark soy sauce. It is good for boiling vegetables and for flavouring delicate dishes, such as clear soup. *Tamari* is a thick soy sauce with a mellow flavour, used as a dip for sashimi and other dishes.

**SUSHI** Different varieties of fresh fish pressed on rice.

*Picture shows (clockwise from left): Mooli, Gobo, Deep Fried tofu, Fresh tofu, Shirataki noodles, Silken tofu and Grilled tofu.*

**SUSHI VINEGAR** Seasoned and sweetened vinegar product for sushi.

**TOFU** Also known as beancurd, this is a soya bean product valued for its high protein content in a vegetarian diet; it is also a good source of calcium and iron. There are several types, including soft or firm tofu; silken tofu; grilled tofu (*yaki-tofu*), or dried tofu. Deep fried tofu, known as *aburage*, is sold ready-made in Japanese shops.

**UMEBOSHI** Small red pickled plums with a sharp and salty taste. Considered as a preservative and used to fill rice balls (*onigiri*).

**WAKAME** Vacuum packed or dried seaweed, for soups and salads.

**WASABI** Green horseradish which tastes extremely hot. Available as a paste or powdered, to which water is added.

# PRAWN TEMPURA

**T**empura is a delicate dish of savoury fritters in light batter. The secret is to use really cold water and to have the oil at the right temperature.

### INGREDIENTS
*8 raw tiger prawns, heads removed*
*oil, for deep frying*
*65g/2¹/₂oz mooli, finely grated and*
*drained, and a shiso leaf, to garnish*

### FOR THE TEMPURA DIP
*200ml/7fl oz/scant 1 cup water*
*45ml/3 tbsp mirin*
*10g/¹/₄oz bonito flakes*
*45ml/3 tbsp soy sauce*

### FOR THE TEMPURA BATTER
*1 egg*
*90ml/6 tbsp iced water*
*75g/3oz/²/₃ cup plain flour*
*2.5ml/¹/₂ tsp baking powder*
*2 ice cubes*

### SERVES 4

---

### COOK'S TIP
Always use Japanese soy sauce in these recipes as Chinese soy sauce tastes much stronger.

---

**1** Carefully shell the tiger prawns, leaving their tails on. Cut one-third of each tail off in a diagonal slit. Press out any excess water with your fingers to prevent it from seeping into the oil and spitting during the cooking process.

**2** Make a shallow cut down the back of each prawn and remove the black intestinal vein.

**3** Lay a prawn on its spine so that it is concave. Using a sharp knife, make three or four diagonal slits into the flesh, about two-thirds of the way in towards the spine, leaving all the pieces attached.

**4** Repeat this process with the remaining prawns. This keeps them straight during cooking. Finally, flatten the prawns with your fingers.

**5** To make the dip, put all the ingredients in a saucepan and bring to the boil. Remove from the heat, leave to cool, and then strain.

**6** Slowly heat the oil for deep frying to 185°C/365°F. Start making the batter when the oil is getting warm.

**7** Always make the batter just before you use it so that it is still very cold. Stir, but do not beat, the egg in a large bowl and set aside half for another use. Add the iced water, flour and baking powder all at once. Stir only two or three times, ignoring the lumps. Add the ice cubes.

**8** Dust the prawns lightly with flour. Hold one by the tail, quickly coat it with batter and slowly lower it into the oil. Do not drop the prawn into the oil as the coating comes off.

**9** Repeat with the remaining prawns, frying them until they rise to the surface of the oil and are crisp. Do not fry until they are golden. Cook a few prawns at a time and then drain them well. Pour the dip into four small bowls. Place the tempura on a plate, garnish with the mooli and shiso leaf and serve immediately.

# SLICED RAW SALMON

**S**liced fresh fish is known as sashimi. This recipe introduces the cutting technique known as *hira zukuri*. Salmon is a good choice for those who have not tried sashimi before because most people are familiar with smoked salmon which is uncooked.

### INGREDIENTS
*2 fresh salmon fillets, skinned and any bones removed, about 400g/14oz total weight*
*soy sauce, to serve*

### FOR THE GARNISH
*50g/2oz/¹/₄ cup mooli*
*20ml/4 tsp wasabi paste*
*shiso leaf*

### SERVES 4

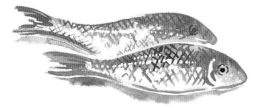

1 Put the salmon fillets in a freezer for about 10 minutes to make them easier to cut, then lay them skinned side up with the thick end to your right and away from you. Tilt the fish to the left.

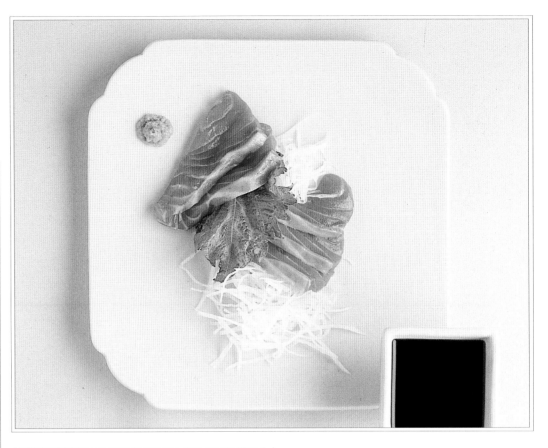

2 Slice the fish towards you, starting the cut from the point of the knife, then slide the slice away from the fillet, to the right. Always slice from the far side towards you.

3 Using a sharp knife, finely shred the mooli. Place it in a large bowl of cold water and leave it for about 5 minutes, then drain it well.

4 Place three slices of prepared salmon on a serving plate, then overlap another two slices on them diagonally. You can arrange fewer or more slices per portion, but an odd number looks better.

5 Garnish each plate of salmon with the finely shredded mooli, wasabi paste and a shiso leaf, then serve the dish immediately with a small bowl of soy sauce as an accompaniment to dip into.

# TERIYAKI TROUT

**T**eriyaki sauce is very useful, not only for fish but also for meat. It is a delicious sweet soy-based sauce that creates a lovely shiny gloss which is very attractive.

### INGREDIENTS
*4 trout fillets*

### FOR THE TERIYAKI MARINADE
*75ml/5 tbsp soy sauce*
*75ml/5 tbsp sake or dry white wine*
*75ml/5 tbsp mirin*

*SERVES 4*

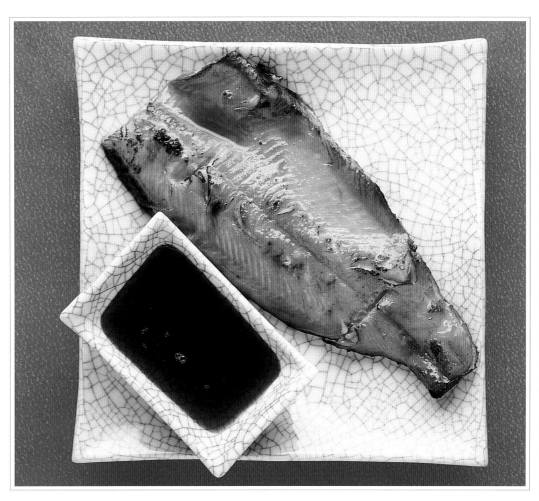

1 Lay the fillets in a shallow dish in a single layer. Mix the marinade ingredients and pour over the fish. Cover and marinate in the fridge for 5–6 hours. Turn occasionally.

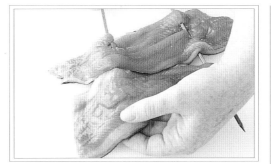

2 Thread two trout fillets neatly together on two metal skewers. Repeat with the remaining two fillets. You could cut the fillets in half if they are too big.

3 Grill the trout fillets on a barbecue over a high heat. Be sure to keep the fish about 10cm/4in away from the flame and brush it with the marinade several times during cooking. Grill each side of the fish until shiny and the trout is cooked through. Alternatively, cook the trout under a conventional grill.

4 Slide the trout off the metal skewers while it is still hot. Serve the fillets either hot or cold with any remaining marinade poured over the top.

# FRIED SWORDFISH

**T**his is a light and tasty cold dish that is suitable for serving on a hot summer's day. Dashi is a stock that provides the underlying flavour for most Japanese dishes.

### INGREDIENTS
*4 swordfish steaks, boned, skin left on,
about 600g/1lb 5oz total weight
15ml/1 tbsp soy sauce
7.5ml/1¹/₂ tsp rice vinegar
bunch of spring onions
4 asparagus spears, trimmed
30ml/2 tbsp oil*

### FOR THE MARINADE
*45ml/3 tbsp soy sauce
45ml/3 tbsp rice vinegar
30ml/2 tbsp sake or dry white wine
15ml/1 tbsp sugar
15ml/1 tbsp instant dashi or water
7.5ml/1¹/₂ tsp sesame oil*

### SERVES 4

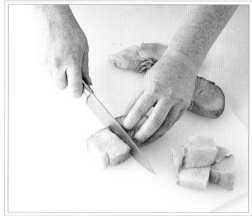

1 Cut the swordfish steaks into 4cm/1½in chunks and place in a dish. Pour the 15ml/1 tbsp soy sauce and 7.5ml/1½ tsp rice vinegar over the fish, then set aside for about 5 minutes. Meanwhile, cut the spring onions into 3cm/1¼in lengths and the asparagus spears into 4cm/1½in lengths.

2 Mix the ingredients for the marinade in a dish. Heat three-quarters of the oil in a frying pan. Wipe the swordfish with kitchen paper and fry over a moderate heat for about 1–2 minutes on each side, or until cooked. Remove the fish from the frying pan and place it in the marinade.

3 Clean the frying pan and heat the remaining oil in it. Fry the spring onions over a moderate heat until browned, then add them to the fish. Fry the asparagus in the oil remaining in the pan over a low heat for 3–4 minutes, then add to the fish.

4 Leave the fish and vegetables to marinate for 10–20 minutes, turning the pieces occasionally. Serve the cold fish with the marinade on a large, deep plate.

# POACHED MACKEREL WITH MISO

This dish, *Mackerel Miso-ni*, is typical of Japanese-style home cooking. There are many types of Japanese miso bean paste, including white miso which is sweet in flavour and dark miso which tastes salty. Darker miso is preferred for this recipe, but you can use any type.

### INGREDIENTS
*1 mackerel, gutted, 675–750g/1¹/₂ –1³/₄lb*
*300ml/¹/₂ pint/1¹/₄ cups instant dashi*
*30ml/2 tbsp sugar*
*60ml/4 tbsp sake or dry white wine*
*10g/¹/₄oz fresh root ginger, peeled and finely sliced*
*115g/4oz/¹/₂ cup miso*
*10g/¹/₄oz fresh root ginger, peeled and finely shredded, to garnish*

*SERVES 4*

### COOK'S TIP
When boiling fish, gently lower it into boiling water. Do not cook it from cold, as the fish will smell unpleasant and the cooking liquid or soup will taste bitter.

1 Chop the head off the mackerel and cut the fish into 2cm/¾in thick steaks. Soak the shredded ginger for the garnish in cold water for 5 minutes, then drain well.

2 Fold a sheet of foil just smaller than the diameter of a large shallow pan. Pour the dashi, sugar and sake or wine into the pan. Bring to the boil, then arrange the mackerel in the pan in a single layer and add the sliced ginger. Spoon the soup over the mackerel, then place the foil over it. Simmer the mackerel for 5–6 minutes.

3 Dissolve the miso in a small mixing bowl in a little of the soup liquid from the saucepan. Carefully pour it back into the saucepan and simmer it for 12 minutes more, spooning the soup over the mackerel occasionally as it cooks.

4 Use a slotted spoon to remove the mackerel carefully from the saucepan and place it on a serving plate. Spoon the remaining soup over the top and garnish the dish with the finely shredded ginger. Serve the mackerel hot.

# CRAB STICK SALAD

In Japan, a couple of small side dishes are often served with a main dish. This is a traditional recipe which harmonizes well within main courses.

### INGREDIENTS
*30g/1¹/₄oz dried wakame seaweed*
*6 crab sticks*
*1 cucumber, about 200g/7oz*
*5ml/1 tsp salt*

### FOR THE VINEGAR DRESSING
*22.5ml/4¹/₂ tsp sugar*
*2ml/¹/₃ tsp salt*
*100ml/3¹/₂fl oz/generous ¹/₃ cup*
*rice vinegar*
*2.5ml/¹/₂ tsp usukuchi soy sauce*

*SERVES 4*

---

### COOK'S TIP
*Usukuchi* soy sauce is light in colour and it has a saltier taste than dark soy sauce, which is stronger and richer in flavour. It is good for boiling vegetables and for flavouring delicate dishes such as clear soup.

---

1 First make the vinegar dressing. Dissolve the sugar and salt thoroughly in the vinegar, then stir in the soy sauce and chill.

2 Soak the dried wakame seaweed in warm water for 5 minutes. Meanwhile, shred the crab sticks.

3 Drain the wakame, cut it into 4cm/1½in long pieces and place in a dish. Cover and chill.

4 Cut the cucumber into 5mm/¼in slices – not too thin or too thick. Dissolve the 5ml/1 tsp salt in 200ml/7fl oz/scant 1 cup water and add the cucumber. Set aside for 5–6 minutes, but to preserve the flavour do not soak it for any longer.

5 Drain the cucumber and dry it on a dish cloth. Wrap the dish cloth around the cucumber and gently squeeze out the water. Then remove the cucumber from the cloth, wrap it in clear film and chill.

6 When you are ready to serve the dish, mix the cucumber with the wakame seaweed and crab sticks, then add the dressing and toss the ingredients lightly together. Serve in four small bowls and pour 15ml/1 tbsp of the dressing over each portion of salad.

# YAKITORI CHICKEN

 *akitori* are Japanese-style chicken kebabs. They are easy to eat and ideal for barbecues or parties.

INGREDIENTS
*6 boneless chicken thighs, with skin*
*bunch of spring onions*
*seven flavour spice, to serve (optional)*

FOR THE YAKITORI SAUCE
*150ml/¹/₄ pint/²/₃ cup soy sauce*
*90g/3¹/₂oz/¹/₂ cup sugar*
*25ml/5 tsp sake or dry white wine*
*15ml/1 tbsp plain flour*

SERVES 4

1 To make the sauce, stir the soy sauce, sugar and sake or wine into the flour in a small pan and bring to the boil, stirring. Reduce the heat and simmer for 10 minutes, until the sauce is reduced by one-third. Then set aside.

2 Cut each chicken thigh into six chunks and cut the spring onions into 3cm/1¼in long pieces.

3 Thread the chicken and spring onions alternately on to 12 bamboo skewers. Grill under a medium heat or on the barbecue, brushing generously several times with the sauce. Grill for 5–10 minutes, until the chicken is cooked but still moist.

4 Serve with a little extra *yakitori* sauce, and sprinkle the kebabs with seven flavour spice, if liked.

# CHICKEN CAKES WITH TERIYAKI SAUCE

hese small chicken cakes, about the size of meatballs, are known in Japanese as *Tsukune*.

### INGREDIENTS
*400g/14oz minced chicken*
*1 size 4 egg*
*60ml/4 tbsp grated onion*
*7.5ml/1½ tsp sugar*
*7.5ml/1½ tsp soy sauce*
*cornflour, for coating*
*15ml/1 tbsp oil*
*½ bunch of spring onions, finely*
*shredded, to garnish*

### FOR THE TERIYAKI SAUCE
*30ml/2 tbsp sake or dry white wine*
*30ml/2 tbsp sugar*
*30ml/2 tbsp mirin*
*30ml/2 tbsp soy sauce*

*SERVES 4*

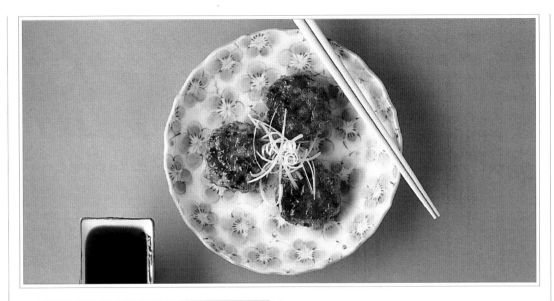

1 Mix the minced chicken with the egg, grated onion, sugar and soy sauce until the ingredients are thoroughly combined and well bound together. This process takes about 3 minutes, until the mixture is quite sticky, which gives a good texture.

2 Shape the mixture into 12 small, flat round cakes and dust them lightly all over with cornflour.

3 Soak the spring onions in a bowl of cold water for 5 minutes and drain well.

4 Heat the oil in a frying pan. Place the chicken cakes in the pan in a single layer, and cook them over a moderate heat for 3 minutes. Turn the cakes over and cook for 3 minutes on the second side.

5 Mix the ingredients for the sauce and pour it into the frying pan. Turn the chicken cakes occasionally until they are evenly glazed with the sauce. Move or gently shake the pan constantly to prevent the sauce from burning.

6 Arrange the chicken cakes on a serving plate and top them with the shredded spring onions. Serve immediately.

# VEGETABLE-STUFFED BEEF ROLLS

T hinly sliced meats are used almost daily in Japanese cooking, so there are countless recipes for them. These stuffed beef rolls, or *Yahata-maki*, are very popular for picnic meals. You can roll up other vegetables in the beef, such as asparagus tips, and you can also replace the beef with pork.

### INGREDIENTS
*50g/2oz carrot*
*50g/2oz green pepper, seeded*
*bunch of spring onions*
*400g/14oz beef topside, thinly sliced*
*plain flour, for dusting*
*15ml/1 tbsp oil*
*fresh parsley sprigs, to garnish*

### FOR THE SAUCE
*30ml/2 tbsp sugar*
*45ml/3 tbsp soy sauce*
*45ml/3 tbsp mirin*

*SERVES 4*

1 Shred the carrot and green pepper into 4–5cm/1½–2in lengths. Halve the spring onions lengthways, then shred them diagonally into similar-size lengths.

2 The beef slices should be 2mm/¹⁄₁₂in thick, no thicker, and about 15cm/6in square. Lay a slice of beef on a chopping board and top it with carrot, green pepper and spring onion strips. Roll it up quite tightly and dust it lightly with flour. Repeat the process with the remaining beef and sliced vegetables.

3 Heat the oil in a frying pan. Add the beef rolls, placing the joins underneath to prevent them from unrolling. Fry them over a moderate heat until golden and cooked, turning occasionally.

4 Add the sauce ingredients to the frying pan and increase the heat. Roll the beef quickly to glaze the rolls.

5 Remove the rolls from the pan and halve them, cutting at a slant. Stand the rolls, with the sloping cut end facing upwards on a plate. Dress with the sauce and garnish with parsley. Serve hot or cold.

# DEEP FRIED PORK STRIPS WITH SHREDDED CABBAGE

**D**eep fried pork is very tasty when served with soft green cabbage and a fruity sauce, known as *tonkatsu*. This dish is enjoyed throughout Japan.

### INGREDIENTS
*4 boneless pork loin steaks, 115g/4oz each*
*7.5ml/1¹/₂ tsp salt*
*freshly ground black pepper*
*plain flour, for coating*
*2 eggs, very lightly beaten*
*50g/2oz fresh white breadcrumbs*
*¹/₂ soft green cabbage, finely shredded*
*oil, for deep frying*

### FOR THE TONKATSU SAUCE
*100ml/3¹/₂fl oz/generous ¹/₃ cup brown sauce (select a fruity brand)*
*45ml/3 tbsp tomato ketchup*
*15ml/1 tbsp sugar*

*SERVES 4*

---

### COOK'S TIP
Commercial Japanese *tonkatsu* sauce is available ready-prepared and it may be substituted for the sauce ingredients listed above.

1 Snip any fat on the pork steaks to ensure that the meat remains flat when frying. Then beat the pork with a meat mallet or a rolling pin to tenderize it. Season with the salt and black pepper, and dust the pork lightly with flour.

2 Dip the steaks into the lightly beaten egg first and then coat them all over with the breadcrumbs. Press the breadcrumbs on to the steaks with your fingers to ensure they stick well. Refrigerate them for about 10 minutes, as chilling will give the coating time to set slightly.

3 Meanwhile, soak the shredded green cabbage in a bowl of cold water for about 5 minutes. Make sure that it is well drained and chill until needed.

4 Mix the ingredients for the *tonkatsu* sauce together in a bowl. Stir constantly and make sure that all the sugar has properly dissolved.

5 Slowly heat the oil for deep frying to 165–170°C/330–340°F. Deep fry two steaks at a time for about 6 minutes, turning them until they are crisp and golden.

6 Skim any floating breadcrumbs from the oil occasionally to prevent them from burning. Drain the steaks well on kitchen towels and keep hot.

7 Cut the steaks into 2cm/³/₄in strips and place them on a plate. Arrange the chilled cabbage beside the pork and pour the sauce over. Serve immediately.

# BEEF AND VEGETABLES ON A HOT PLATE

**T**his is *Yakiniku*, a dish of beef cooked at the table – you will need a portable griddle or grill pan and you can cook a variety of different ingredients, such as chicken or fish.

### INGREDIENTS

*1 oak leaf lettuce*
*1 mooli, finely grated*
*oil, for cooking*
*400g/14oz beef topside, very thinly sliced*
*1 red pepper, seeded and sliced*
*1 green pepper, seeded and sliced*
*1 large mild onion, sliced into rings*
*4 shiitake mushrooms, stems removed*
*1 carrot, thinly sliced*
*8 raw tiger prawns, heads removed,*
*shelled, with tails left on*
*soy sauce, to serve*

### FOR THE PONZU DIP
*100ml/3¹/₂fl oz/generous ¹/₃ cup each of*
*lemon juice, soy sauce and instant dashi*

### SERVES 4

**1** Prepare the dip by mixing all the ingredients. Divide the dip among four small individual serving bowls. Separate the lettuce leaves and arrange them on plates.

**2** Gently squeeze the grated mooli to remove any excess water. Place 15–30ml/1–2 tbsp mooli into four small individual serving bowls and pour on a little soy sauce.

**3** Heat the grill or a hot plate on a thick mat to protect the table. Add a little oil and quickly grill the beef until it is cooked on both sides. Grill the peppers, onion, shiitake mushrooms, carrot and prawns at the same time.

**4** To eat the food, wrap individual portions in lettuce leaves and dip them into the ponzu or mooli dip. Alternatively, the food may be dipped without being wrapped in the lettuce leaves if preferred.

### COOK'S TIP
This recipe is an example of a party meal, an essential part of Japanese home entertainment. Dishes are cooked at the table so guests can participate in cooking their own food.

# SPINACH WITH BONITO FLAKES

**T**his is a cold side dish of lightly cooked spinach dressed with fine bonito flakes. A similar vegetarian side dish can be prepared by omitting the bonito flakes and marinating the spinach in kombu seaweed stock and soy sauce.

### INGREDIENTS
*300g/11oz whole spinach, roots trimmed*

### FOR THE MARINADE
*60ml/4 tbsp kombu and bonito stock or instant dashi*
*20ml/4 tsp* usukuchi *soy sauce*
*60ml/4 tbsp fine bonito flakes*
(katsuo bushi)

*SERVES 4*

1 Wash the spinach thoroughly. Keeping the stems together, hold the leaves of the spinach and lower the stems into boiling water for 10 seconds before lowering the leaves into the water and boiling for about 1–2 minutes. Do not overcook the spinach.

2 Meanwhile, prepare a large bowl of cold water. Drain the spinach and soak it in the cold water for 1 minute to preserve its colour and remove any bitterness.

3 Drain the spinach and squeeze it well, holding the stems upwards and squeezing firmly down the length of the spinach leaves.

4 Mix the stock and soy sauce in a dish and marinate the spinach in this mixture for 10–15 minutes, turning it over once.

5 Squeeze the spinach lightly and cut it into 3–4cm/1¼ –1½in long pieces, reserving the marinade. Divide the spinach among four small bowls, arranging the pieces so that the cut edges face upwards. Sprinkle 15ml/1 tbsp bonito flakes and a little of the marinade over each portion, then serve immediately.

# MOOLI WITH SESAME MISO SAUCE

**T**his simple vegetable dish makes a good starter. The rice is added to keep the mooli white and to remove any bitterness from the vegetables.

### INGREDIENTS
*1 mooli, about 800g/1³⁄₄lb*
*15ml/1 tbsp rice, washed*
*salt, to taste*
*1 sheet kombu seaweed,*
*20 x 10cm/8 x 4in*
*punnet of cress, to garnish*

### FOR THE SESAME MISO SAUCE
*75g/3oz/generous ¹⁄₃ cup each red and*
*white miso paste*
*60ml/4 tbsp mirin*
*30ml/2 tbsp sugar*
*20ml/4 tsp ground white sesame seeds*

### SERVES 4

1 Slice the mooli into 2cm/¾in thick slices, then peel off the skin. Wrap the rice in a piece of muslin or cheesecloth and tie with string, allowing room for the rice to expand during cooking. Place the mooli, rice bag and some salt in a pan, fill with water and bring to the boil. Simmer for 15 minutes. Gently drain the mooli and discard the rice.

2 Place the seaweed in a large pan, lay the mooli on top and fill with water. Bring to the boil, then simmer for 20 minutes.

3 Meanwhile, make the sauce. Mix the red and white miso pastes together in a saucepan. Add the mirin and sugar, simmer for 5–6 minutes, and make sure that you stir continuously. Remove from the heat and add the sesame seeds.

4 Arrange the mooli and seaweed in a large dish with their hot cooking stock. Sprinkle cress over the top. Serve the mooli on small plates with the sesame miso sauce poured over and garnished with some of the cress. The seaweed is used only to flavour the mooli and is not eaten.

# JAPANESE-STYLE POTATO SALAD

**F**or this salad, the potatoes are first stir-fried with carrots and onion, then cooked in stock before some beaten egg is added.

INGREDIENTS

4 potatoes

2 carrots

1 large mild onion

20ml/4 tsp oil

1 vegetable stock cube

20ml/4 tsp rice vinegar

10ml/2 tsp sugar

2.5ml/$^1$/$_2$ tsp salt, plus extra for cucumber

2 size 4 eggs, beaten

$^1$/$_2$ cucumber

SERVES 4

1 Cut the potatoes lengthways into four, then slice the pieces across into thick chunks. Soak the potatoes in cold water for 2 minutes and drain well.

2 Halve the carrots vertically, then slice them across into chunks. Cut the onion into thick wedges.

3 Heat the oil in a deep frying pan or in a saucepan. Stir-fry the chopped potatoes, carrots and onion wedges for 1 minute. Dissolve the vegetable stock cube in 200ml/7fl oz/scant 1 cup boiling water and pour it into the saucepan.

4 Add the rice vinegar, sugar and salt to the pan. Cover and simmer for about 5 minutes. Remove the lid from the pan and continue to cook the vegetables over a moderate heat until all the liquid has evaporated. Shake the pan gently now and again to prevent the vegetables from sticking to the pan as the liquid dries up.

5 Remove from the heat and allow to cool for 30 seconds, then add the beaten egg and stir quickly until the egg sets. Transfer to a dish and leave to cool, then chill.

6 Meanwhile, halve the cucumber vertically and cut it into thin slices. Place the cucumber in a colander or sieve over a bowl. Sprinkle with a little salt and leave to stand for 10 minutes. Gently squeeze out the liquid from the cucumber.

7 Add the cucumber to the potato mixture and check the seasoning, adding more salt, if necessary. Serve chilled.

# FRENCH BEANS WITH SESAME SEEDS

This excellent vegetarian dish is flavoured with a delicious Gomaae sauce made predominantly from sesame seeds. Serve it with other vegetables, such as spinach, if you like.

INGREDIENTS
*200g/7oz French beans*
*salt*

FOR THE GOMAAE SAUCE
*60ml/4 tbsp white sesame seeds*
*10ml/2 tsp sugar*
*15ml/1 tbsp soy sauce*
*15ml/1 tbsp instant dashi*

SERVES 4

1 Top and tail the French beans and then cook them in boiling salted water for about 2 minutes, or until they are tender.

2 Drain the cooked beans and soak them in cold water for 1 minute to preserve their colour. Drain well and cut into lengths of 3–4cm/1¼–1½ in. Chill for 5 minutes.

3 To make the sauce, grind the white sesame seeds in a pestle and mortar, leaving some of the sesame seeds whole. Alternatively, roughly chop the sesame seeds on a chopping board with a knife.

4 Put the ground white sesame seeds into a small mixing bowl and carefully stir in the sugar. Then add the soy sauce and the instant dashi. Mix all the ingredients together well with a rubber spatula.

5 To serve, put the chilled French beans in a large mixing bowl, add the sauce and toss well. Transfer the beans to four small bowls, and serve immediately.

# ROLLED OMELETTE

**T**his is a firmly set Rolled Omelette, which is cut into neat pieces and can be served hot or cold. The texture should be smooth and soft, not leathery, and the flavour is sweet-savoury. Mooli and soy sauce are perfect condiments to complement its flavour and texture.

INGREDIENTS
*8 eggs*
*60ml/4 tbsp sugar*
*20ml/4 tsp soy sauce*
*90ml/6 tbsp sake or dry white wine*
*vegetable oil, for cooking*
*soy sauce, to serve*

FOR THE GARNISH
*8cm/3¼in length of mooli, finely grated*
*lettuce leaves*
gari *(ginger pickles)*

SERVES 4

1 Break the eggs into a large mixing bowl. Do not beat the eggs, but mix them together by stirring them with a pair of chopsticks, using a cutting action.

2 Mix the sugar with the soy sauce and sake or wine in a small bowl. Lightly stir this mixture into the eggs. Pour half the mixture into another bowl as the omelette will be cooked in two equal batches.

3 Heat a little oil in a frying pan and wipe off the excess with kitchen paper.

4 Pour a quarter of the egg mixture from one bowl into the frying pan, tilting the pan to coat it with a thin layer. When the edge has set, but the middle is still moist, roll up the egg towards you.

5 Moisten some kitchen paper with oil and grease the empty side of the frying pan. Pour a third of the remaining egg mixture into the frying pan. Lift the rolled egg up with the chopsticks and let the raw egg run underneath it.

6 When the edge has set, but the middle is still moist, roll up the omelette in the opposite direction, tilting the pan away from you so that the egg rolls easily.

7 Slide the omelette roll towards you again, grease the frying pan and pour half of the remaining mixture on to it, allowing the egg to run under the roll as before. When set, insert the chopsticks in the side of the rolled omelette, then flip it over towards the opposite side of the pan. Add the remaining egg from the first batch and cook as before.

8 Slide the roll so that its join is underneath. Cook for 10 seconds.

9 Slide the roll out on to a bamboo mat and roll up tightly, then press neatly into a rectangular shape. Leave to cool. Cook the second batch of egg mixture in the same way. Slice the cold omelettes into 2.5cm/1in thick pieces and garnish with mooli, lettuce and *gari*. Serve with soy sauce.

# SALMON SEALED WITH EGG

**T**amago-toji, meaning egg cover, is the Japanese title for this type of dish which can be made from various ingredients. Canned pink salmon is used here for a very delicate flavour. Fried tofu can be used instead of salmon.

### INGREDIENTS
*400g/14oz can pink salmon, drained,*
*bones and skin removed*
*10 mangetouts, trimmed*
*2 large mild onions, sliced*
*40ml/8 tsp sugar*
*30ml/2 tbsp soy sauce*
*4 size 4 eggs, beaten*

*SERVES 4*

1 Flake the canned salmon. Boil the trimmed mangetouts for 2–3 minutes, drain and slice finely.

2 Put the sliced onions in a frying pan, add 200ml/7fl oz/scant 1 cup water and bring to the boil. Cook for 5 minutes over a moderate heat, then add the sugar and soy sauce. Cook for a further 5 minutes.

3 Add the flaked salmon and cook for 2–3 minutes, or until the soup has virtually evaporated. Pour the egg over to cover the surface. Sprinkle in the mangetouts and cover the pan. Cook for 1 minute over a moderate heat, until just set. Do not overcook or the eggs will curdle and separate. Spoon on to a plate from the pan and serve immediately.

# TOFU STEAKS

**T**ofu was originally introduced from China. High in protein and low in fat, it readily absorbs the flavours of the dish in which it is used. It can be eaten raw, deep fried or stewed. Vegetarians and those who eat meat will equally enjoy these tasty tofu steaks.

### INGREDIENTS
*300g/11oz fresh Japanese tofu,*
*10 x 8 x 3cm/4 x 3¹/₄ x 1¹/₄in*
*30ml/2 tbsp oil*
*2 spring onions, thinly sliced and mixed salad leaves, to garnish*
*seven flavour spice, to serve (optional)*

### FOR THE MARINADE
*45ml/3 tbsp sake*
*30ml/2 tbsp* usukuchi *soy sauce*
*5ml/1 tsp sesame oil*
*1 garlic clove, crushed*
*15ml/1 tbsp grated fresh root ginger*
*1 spring onion, finely chopped*

### SERVES 4

1 Wrap the tofu in a dish cloth and place it on a chopping board. Put a large plate on the top and leave the tofu for 30 minutes to remove any excess water.

2 Slice the strained tofu horizontally into three pieces, then cut the slices into quarters. Thoroughly mix the ingredients for the marinade in a large dish. Add the tofu chunks in a single layer and set aside for 30 minutes to absorb the flavours.

3 Heat half the oil in a frying pan and cook half the tofu steaks. Fry over a moderate heat for 3 minutes on each side, or until golden. Repeat with the other steaks.

4 Arrange three tofu steaks on each plate. Heat any remaining marinade as it may be poured over the steaks. Sprinkle with the spring onions and garnish with mixed salad leaves. Serve immediately with seven flavour spice, if liked.

# DEEP FRIED TOFU AND ASPARAGUS IN STOCK

**A**gedashi is the name for dishes of deep fried *(age)* ingredients served in a stock *(dashi)* or thin sauce. Here, deep fried tofu and asparagus are served in a thin stock-based sauce and topped with tomato. A cup of sake goes very well with this *Agedashi*.

### INGREDIENTS
*200g/7oz fresh Japanese tofu,*
*10 x 5 x 3cm/4 x 2 x 1¹/₄in*
*4 asparagus spears, trimmed of tough*
*stalk ends*
*1 beef tomato, skinned*
*oil, for deep frying*
*cornflour, for coating*

### FOR THE SAUCE
*200ml/7fl oz/scant 1 cup instant dashi*
*50ml/2fl oz/¹/₄ cup mirin*
*50ml/2fl oz/¹/₄ cup soy sauce*

### SERVES 4

1 Wrap the tofu in a kitchen towel and press between two plates for 30 minutes, removing any excess moisture. Alternatively, wrap the tofu in kitchen paper, place it on a plate and cook it in the microwave for 1 minute (600W). Cut the tofu into eight cubes, each measuring about 2.5cm/1in.

2 Cut the asparagus into 3–4cm/1¼–1½in lengths. Halve the tomato and remove the seeds, then cut it into 5mm/¼in cubes.

3 Slowly heat the oil for deep frying to a temperature of 170°C/340°F. Coat the tofu with cornflour.

4 Deep fry the tofu pieces in two batches over a medium heat until golden, allowing 7–10 minutes to ensure that the tofu is cooked thoroughly. It starts to expand once it is cooked. Drain well. Keep the oil temperature at 170°C/340°F during cooking.

5 Meanwhile, place the ingredients for the sauce in a saucepan and bring to the boil, then simmer gently for 3 minutes. Deep fry the asparagus lengths for 2 minutes and drain them well.

6 Place the tofu on a large plate and arrange the asparagus on top. Pour on the hot sauce and sprinkle the tomato on top. Serve immediately.

# BOILED FRIED TOFU WITH HIJIKI SEAWEED

oiled dishes, known as *nimono*, are enjoyed throughout the year in Japanese homes.

### INGREDIENTS
*20g/³/₄oz dried hijiki seaweed*
*1 sheet Japanese fried tofu (aburage)*
*30g/1¹/₄oz carrot*
*30g/1¹/₄oz fresh shiitake mushrooms,*
*stems removed*
*15ml/1 tbsp oil*
*100ml/3¹/₂fl oz/generous ¹/₃ cup*
*instant dashi*
*22.5ml/4¹/₂ tsp sake or dry white wine*
*15ml/1 tbsp mirin*
*22.5ml/4¹/₂ tsp soy sauce*
*22.5ml/4¹/₂ tsp sugar*

### SERVES 4

1 Wash the hijiki seaweed and soak it in cold water for 30 minutes. Drain well. Do not soak for any longer as it will lack flavour. During soaking, the hijiki will expand to about six times its dried volume.

2 Put the tofu in a strainer and rinse with hot water from a kettle to remove any excess oil. Shred it to 3cm/1¼in lengths. Shred the carrot and shiitake mushrooms into strips of about the same size.

3 Heat the oil in a large pan. Add the carrot, stir once, then add the shiitake mushrooms and stir-fry over a high heat for 1 minute. Add the hijiki, stir, then add the fried tofu and stir-fry for 1 minute.

4 Pour in the dashi, sake or wine, mirin and soy sauce. Stir in the sugar. Bring to the boil and reduce the heat, then simmer until all the soup has evaporated, stirring occasionally. Serve the tofu hot or cold, in four small bowls.

### COOK'S TIP
Hijiki is a dried seaweed with a high fibre content. If Japanese fried tofu is not available, Chinese fried tofu may be used instead.

# Winter Tofu and Vegetables

T his dish is brought bubbling hot to the table with a pot of dip to accompany the freshly cooked tofu and vegetables.

### Ingredients
*1 sheet kombu seaweed,*
*20 x 10cm/8 x 4in*
*600g/1lb 5oz Japanese silken tofu,*
*10 x 8 x 3cm/4 x 3¹/₄ x 1¹/₄in*
*2 leeks*
*4 shiitake mushrooms, cross cut in top*
*and stems removed*
*spring onions, to garnish*

### For the Dip
*200ml/7fl oz/scant 1 cup soy sauce*
*generous 15ml/1 tbsp mirin*
*100ml/3¹/₂fl oz/generous ¹/₃ cup*
*bonito flakes*

### Serves 4

1 Half fill a large flameproof casserole or saucepan with cold water and soak the kombu seaweed in it for 30 minutes.

2 Cut the silken tofu into 4cm/1½in cubes. Slice the leeks diagonally into 2cm/¾in thick slices.

3 To make the dip, bring the soy sauce and mirin to the boil, then add the bonito flakes. Remove from the heat and leave until all the flakes have sunk to the bottom of the pan, then strain the sauce and pour it into a small heatproof basin.

4 Stand the basin in the middle of the pan, placing it on an upturned saucer, if necessary, so that it is well above the level of the water. This keeps the dip hot. Bring the water to the boil.

5 Add the mushrooms and leeks to the pan, and cook for about 5 minutes over a moderate heat until softened. Then gently add the tofu. When the tofu starts floating, it is ready to eat. If the tofu won't all fit in the pan, it can be added during the meal.

6 Take the pan to the table and spoon the dip into four small bowls. Sprinkle the spring onions into the dip. Diners help themselves to tofu and vegetables from the pan and eat them with the dip. The kombu seaweed is used only to flavour the dish; it is not eaten.

# MIXED RICE

**R**ice is a staple part of the Japanese diet and this is one of the many ways of cooking it. This recipe makes a very good party dish, and you can add a variety of ingredients to create your own special version. *Aburage*, a deep fried tofu, is sold ready-made in Japanese shops.

### INGREDIENTS
*6 dried shiitake mushrooms*
*2 sheets fried tofu* (aburage), *each*
*13 x 6cm/5 x 2¹/₂in*
*6 mangetouts*
*1 carrot, cut into matchstick strips*
*115g/4oz chicken fillet, diced*
*30ml/2 tbsp sugar*
*37.5ml/7¹/₂ tsp soy sauce*
*salt*
*1kg/2¹/₄lb/7 cups freshly boiled*
*Japanese rice*

### SERVES 4

1 Soak the dried shiitake mushrooms in 800ml/27fl oz/3¹/₂ cups water for about 30 minutes. Place a small plate or saucer on top of the mushrooms to keep them submerged during soaking.

2 Put the fried tofu into a strainer and pour over hot water from a kettle to remove any excess fat. Squeeze the tofu and cut it in half lengthways, then slice it into 5mm/¹/₄in wide strips.

3 Boil the mangetouts, then drain and refresh them in cold water. Drain well. Shred the mangetouts finely.

4 Drain the shiitake mushrooms, reserving the soaking water, and carefully remove their stems. Using a sharp knife, finely slice the mushroom caps. Pour the soaking water into a saucepan and add the tofu, carrots, chicken and shiitake mushrooms.

5 Bring the ingredients to the boil, then skim the broth and simmer for about 1–2 minutes. Add the sugar and cook for 1 minute, then add the soy sauce and salt. Simmer gently until most of the liquid has evaporated, leaving only a small amount of concentrated broth.

6 Mix in the boiled hot rice, sprinkle the mangetouts over the top and serve the mixed rice at once.

# RICE BALLS

Picnics are very popular in Japan and rice balls, or *Onigiri*, make an ideal dish. You can put anything you like in the rice, so you could invent your own. *Yaki-nori* are a ready-made version of dried seaweed sheets.

### INGREDIENTS
*1kg/2¹/₄lb/7 cups freshly boiled*
*Japanese rice*
*4 umeboshi (plum pickles)*
*15ml/1 tbsp salt*
*1 salmon steak, grilled*
*¹/₂ sheet* yaki-nori *seaweed*
*15ml/1 tbsp white or black sesame seeds*
*cucumber slices and cress, to garnish*

*SERVES 4 (8 RICE BALLS)*

---

### COOK'S TIP
Always use hot rice to make these balls, then allow them to cool completely before wrapping each one in clear film or foil.

---

1 Spoon one-eighth of the rice into a small rice bowl. Make a hole in the middle and put in one umeboshi. Cover with rice. Put the salt in a bowl.

2 Wet the palms of both hands with cold water, put a finger into the salt bowl and rub the salt evenly on to your palms.

3 Place the rice and umeboshi ball on one hand. Use both hands to shape the rice into a triangle, using firm but not heavy pressure. Make three more rice triangles.

4 Flake the salmon, discarding the skin and bones. Mix the fish into the remaining rice, then shape it into triangles as before.

5 Cut the *yaki-nori* into four strips and wrap one round each of the rice balls. Sprinkle sesame seeds on the rice balls and garnish with cucumber and cress.

# STEAK BOWL

This appetizing dish looks very good at a dinner party and it is also very easy to prepare, leaving the cook with time to relax.

INGREDIENTS
*1 large mild onion*
*1 red pepper, seeded*
*30ml/2 tbsp oil*
*30ml/2 tbsp butter*
*400g/14oz sirloin steak, trimmed of excess fat*
*60ml/4 tbsp tomato ketchup*
*30ml/2 tbsp Worcestershire sauce*
*30ml/2 tbsp chopped parsley*
*1kg/2¹/₄lb/7 cups freshly boiled Japanese rice*
*salt and freshly ground black pepper*
*bunch of watercress, to garnish*

SERVES 4

1 Cut the onion and red pepper into 7–8mm/⅓in slices.

2 Heat 15ml/1 tbsp of the oil in a frying pan and cook the onion slices until golden on both sides, adding salt and pepper, then set aside.

3 Heat the remaining oil and 15ml/1 tbsp of the butter. Cook the steak over a high heat until browned on both sides, then cut it into bite-size pieces and set aside. For well-done steak, cook it over a moderate heat for 1–2 minutes on each side.

4 Mix the tomato ketchup, Worcestershire sauce and 30ml/2 tbsp water in the pan in which the steak was cooked. Stir over a moderate heat for 1 minute, mixing in the meat residue.

5 Mix the remaining butter and the chopped parsley into the hot rice. Divide among four serving bowls. Top the rice with the red pepper, onion and steak, and pour over the sauce. Garnish with watercress.

# CHILLED NOODLES

T hese classic Japanese cold noodles are known as *somen*. The noodles are surprisingly refreshing when eaten with the accompanying ingredients and a delicately flavoured dip. The noodles are served with ice to ensure that they remain chilled until they are eaten.

### INGREDIENTS
*oil, for cooking*
*2 size 4 eggs, beaten with a pinch of salt*
*1 sheet* yaki-nori *seaweed, finely shredded*
*¹/₂ bunch of spring onions, sliced*
*20ml/4 tsp wasabi paste*
*400g/14oz dried* somen *noodles*
*ice cubes, to serve*

### FOR THE DIP
*1 litre/1³/₄ pints/4 cups kombu and*
*bonito stock or instant dashi*
*200ml/7fl oz/scant 1 cup soy sauce*
*15ml/1 tbsp mirin*

### SERVES 4

1 Prepare the dip in advance so that it has time to cool and chill. Bring the ingredients to the boil, then leave to cool and chill thoroughly.

2 Heat a little oil in a frying pan. Pour in half the beaten eggs, tilting the pan to coat the base evenly. Leave the egg to set, then turn it over and cook the second side briefly. Turn the omelette out on to a board. Cook the remaining egg in the same way.

3 Leave the omelettes to cool and then shred them finely. Divide the shredded omelette, *yaki-nori*, spring onions and wasabi among four small bowls.

4 Boil the *somen* noodles according to the packet instructions and drain. Rinse the noodles in or under cold running water, stirring with chopsticks, then drain well.

5 Place the cooked noodles on a large plate and add some ice cubes on top to keep them cool.

6 Pour the cold dip into four more small bowls. The noodles and the selected accompaniments are dipped into the chilled dip before they are eaten.

# FIVE-FLAVOUR NOODLES

he Japanese title for this dish is *Gomoku Yakisoba*, meaning five different ingredients.

### INGREDIENTS
*300g/11oz dried Chinese thin egg noodles or 500g/1¹/₄lb fresh yakisoba noodles*
*200g/7oz lean boneless pork, thinly sliced*
*22.5ml/4¹/₂ tsp oil*
*10g/¹/₄oz fresh root ginger, grated*
*1 garlic clove, crushed*
*200g/7oz/1³/₄ cups green cabbage, roughly chopped*
*115g/4oz/¹/₂ cup beansprouts*
*1 green pepper, seeded and cut into fine strips*
*1 red pepper, seeded and cut into fine strips*
*salt and white pepper*
*20ml/4 tsp ao-nori seaweed, to garnish (optional)*

### FOR THE SEASONING
*60ml/4 tbsp Worcestershire sauce*
*15ml/1 tbsp soy sauce*
*15ml/1 tbsp oyster sauce*
*15ml/1 tbsp sugar*
*2.5ml/¹/₂ tsp salt*

*SERVES 4*

1 Boil the noodles according to the packet instructions and drain. Cut the pork into 3–4cm/1¹/₄–1¹/₂in strips and season with salt and white pepper.

2 Heat 7.5ml/1¹/₂ tsp oil in a large frying pan or a wok and stir-fry the pork until just cooked, then remove it from the pan.

3 Wipe the pan with kitchen paper, and then heat the remaining oil in it. Add the ginger, garlic and cabbage and stir-fry for 1 minute.

4 Add the beansprouts and stir until softened, then add the green and red peppers and stir-fry for 1 minute.

5 Replace the pork in the pan and add the noodles. Stir in all the seasoning ingredients and more white pepper if you like. Stir-fry for 2–3 minutes.

6 Serve immediately, sprinkled with the *ao-nori* seaweed, if liked.

# INDIVIDUAL NOODLE CASSEROLES

**T**raditionally, these individual casseroles are cooked in separate earthenware pots. *Nabe* means pot and *yaki* means to heat, providing the Japanese title of *Nabeyaki Udon* for this exciting recipe.

### INGREDIENTS
*115g/4oz boneless chicken thigh*
*2.5ml/¹/₂ tsp salt*
*2.5ml/¹/₂ tsp sake or dry white wine*
*2.5ml/¹/₂ tsp soy sauce*
*1 leek*
*115g/4oz whole spinach, trimmed*
*300g/11oz dried udon noodles or*
*500g/1¹/₄lb fresh*
*4 shiitake mushrooms, stems removed*
*4 size 4 eggs*
*seven flavour spice, to serve (optional)*

### FOR THE SOUP
*1.4 litres/2¹/₃ pints/6 cups kombu and*
*bonito stock or instant dashi*
*22.5ml/4¹/₂ tsp soy sauce*
*7ml/1¹/₃ tsp salt*
*15ml/1 tbsp mirin*

*SERVES 4*

1 Cut the chicken thigh into small chunks and sprinkle with the salt, sake or wine and soy sauce. Cut the leek diagonally into 1.5cm/1¾in slices.

2 Boil the spinach for 2 minutes. Drain and soak in cold water for 1 minute. Drain, squeeze and cut into 4cm/1½in lengths.

3 Boil the dried *udon* noodles according to the packet instructions, allowing 3 minutes less than the suggested cooking time. If using fresh *udon* noodles, place them in boiling water, disentangle the noodles well and then drain them.

---

### COOK'S TIP
Prawn tempura could be served in these casseroles instead of chicken and egg.

---

4 Bring the ingredients for the soup to the boil in a saucepan and add the chicken and leeks. Skim the broth, then cook it for 5 minutes.

5 Divide the *udon* noodles among four individual flameproof casseroles. Pour the soup, chicken and leeks into the casseroles. Place over a moderate heat, then add the shiitake mushrooms.

6 Gently break an egg into each casserole. Cover and simmer for 2 minutes. Divide the spinach among the casseroles and simmer for 1 minute.

7 Serve immediately, standing the hot casseroles on plates or table mats. Sprinkle seven flavour spice over the casseroles, if liked.

# SHAPED SUSHI

his exciting and fresh sushi dish includes some sashimi, which are slices of raw fish.

### INGREDIENTS
*480g/1lb 1oz/2¹/₄ cups Japanese rice,*
*washed and drained for 1 hour*
*30ml/2 tbsp sake or dry white wine*
*1 Rolled Omelette*
*5ml/1 tsp wasabi paste*
*soy sauce,* gari *and lettuce, to serve*

### FOR THE SUSHI VINEGAR
*60ml/4 tbsp rice vinegar*
*15ml/1 tbsp sugar*
*5ml/1 tsp salt*

### FOR THE SEAFOOD GARNISH
*1 squid body sack, skinned, about*
*200g/7oz total weight*
*1 leg boiled octopus*
*200g/7oz block tuna for sashimi*
*200g/7oz block salmon for sashimi*
*4 raw prawns with shells, heads removed*

### FOR THE MARINADE
*15ml/1 tbsp rice vinegar*
*5ml/1 tsp sugar*
*pinch of salt*

*SERVES 4*

1 Cook the rice, replacing 30ml/2 tbsp of the measured cooking water with the sake or wine.

2 Meanwhile, heat the ingredients for the sushi vinegar, stir well and cool. Add this to the hot cooked rice, stir well with a spatula, at the same time fanning the rice constantly – this gives the rice an attractive glaze. Cover with a damp dish cloth and leave to cool. Do not put in the fridge, as this will make the rice go hard.

3 Cut the squid into strips measuring 2–3cm/³/₄–1¹/₄in wide and 5cm/2in long. Carefully, slice the octopus leg into strips of the same size. Cut the block tuna and salmon into pieces of similar size, about 3mm/¹/₈in thick.

4 Thread the prawns on bamboo skewers from tail to head to make sure they lie flat when cooked. Boil for 1 minute, then remove the skewers and shells, leaving the tails intact. Slit each prawn along the belly, taking care not to cut through, and remove the dark vein. Open each one up like a book.

5 Mix the marinade ingredients in a dish, add the prawns and leave aside for about 10 minutes.

6 Slice the Rolled Omelette into 5mm/¹/₄in thick pieces.

7 Wet your hands with some cold water, and then carefully shape about 15–20g/¹/₂–³/₄oz rice into a rectangle measuring 1cm/¹/₂in high, 2cm/³/₄in wide and 5cm/2in long. Repeat this process with the remaining rice.

8 Use your finger to spread a little wasabi paste on to the middle of each rice rectangle and divide the seafood among the rectangles, laying them on top. Do not add wasabi paste for egg sushi.

9 Serve the sushi immediately, with soy sauce, *gari* and lettuce. The *gari* may be eaten to cleanse the palate after each mouthful, if liked.

# TOFU-WRAPPED SUSHI

**I**nari-sushi is another popular picnic dish. It uses *aburage*, a deep fried tofu that is ideal for stuffing. The tofu should be prepared while the rice is cooking (or beforehand) as the rice has to be warm so that it can be packed into the tofu.

### INGREDIENTS
6 sheets fried tofu (aburage)
200ml/7fl oz/scant 1 cup kombu and
bonito stock or instant dashi
45ml/3 tbsp sugar
37.5ml/7¹/₂ tsp soy sauce
30ml/2 tbsp sake or dry white wine
30ml/2 tbsp mirin
dash of rice vinegar
gari (ginger pickles), to garnish

### FOR THE RICE
240g/8¹/₂oz/1¹/₈ cups Japanese rice
15ml/1 tbsp sake

### FOR THE SUSHI VINEGAR
30ml/2 tbsp rice vinegar
15ml/1 tbsp sugar
2.5ml/¹/₂ tsp salt

*MAKES 12*

1 Lay a sheet of fried tofu on a board. Using a chopstick as a rolling pin, roll the tofu as this will ensure that it opens easily when boiled. Bring a large saucepan of water to the boil and blanch the tofu to remove any excess fat, then drain and squeeze it. Cut the sheets of tofu in half widthways, then carefully open out with a knife to make 12 small sacks or pockets.

2 Bring the stock, sugar, soy sauce, sake or wine, mirin and rice vinegar to the boil. Add the tofu, cover with folded foil and simmer until the liquid has virtually evaporated, pressing the foil down occasionally to squeeze the soup from the tofu and prevent the packets from filling. Drain and cool. Heat the ingredients for the sushi vinegar and leave to cool.

3 Cook the rice, replacing 15ml/1 tbsp of the measured cooking water with the sake. Add the sushi vinegar to the rice and stir well with a spatula. Divide the warm rice between the tofu and fold the tofu to enclose the rice in neat parcels. Arrange on plates with the folded sides underneath and serve garnished with *gari*.

# TUNA RICE BOWL

ne of the most popular dishes in Japan, *Tekka-don* consists of rice with fresh tuna laid on top.

### INGREDIENTS
*480g/1lb 1oz/2¼ cups Japanese rice, washed and drained for 1 hour*
*30ml/2 tbsp sake or dry white wine*
*300g/11oz block tuna for sashimi*
*1 sheet* yaki-nori *seaweed*
*lettuce and 20ml/4 tsp wasabi paste, to garnish*
*soy sauce, to serve*

### SERVES 4

1 Cook the rice, replacing 30ml/2 tbsp of the measured cooking water with the sake or wine.

2 Cut thin slices of tuna, tilting it to the side. Cut towards you from the far side.

3 Using scissors, cut the *yaki-nori* seaweed very carefully into 5cm/2in size pieces in length.

4 The rice must be at room temperature, so as not to cook the tuna. Divide it among four bowls.

5 Arrange the tuna on top of the rice and sprinkle the seaweed gently over the top. Garnish with lettuce and 5ml/1 tsp of the wasabi paste for each plate, and serve immediately with soy sauce.

# SIMPLE ROLLED SUSHI

To perfect the art of rolling sushi in seaweed, start with this simple form of rolled sushi known as *Hosomaki*, which is usually a slim roll with only one filling. You will need a bamboo mat *(makisu)* for the rolling process.

### INGREDIENTS
*6 sheets* yaki-nori *seaweed*
gari *(ginger pickles), to garnish*
*soy sauce, to serve*

### FOR THE FILLING
*200g/7oz block tuna for sashimi*
*200g/7oz block salmon for sashimi*
*30ml/2 tbsp wasabi paste*
*¹/₂ cucumber, quartered lengthways and seeds removed*

### FOR THE RICE
*400g/14oz/2 cups Japanese rice, washed and drained for 1 hour*
*25ml/5 tsp sake or dry white wine*

### FOR THE MIXED VINEGAR
*52.5ml/10¹/₂ tsp rice vinegar*
*15ml/1 tbsp sugar*
*3ml/²/₃ tsp salt*

*MAKES 12 ROLLS OR 72 SLICES*

1 Cook the rice, replacing 25ml/5 tsp of the measured cooking water with the sake or wine. Heat the ingredients for the vinegar, stir well and cool. Add the rice.

2 Cut the *yaki-nori* in half lengthways. Cut the fish into four 1cm/½in sauare stickes, the length of the long side of the *nori*. Use two sticks per *nori* if necessary.

3 Place a sheet of *nori*, shiny side downwards, on a bamboo mat on a chopping board.

4 Divide the rice in half in its bowl. Mark each half into six, making 12 portions in all. Spread one portion of the rice over the *nori* with your fingers, leaving a 1cm/½in space uncovered at the top and bottom of the *nori*.

5 Spread a little wasabi in a horizontal line along the middle of the rice and lay a stick of tuna on this.

6 Holding the mat and the edge of the *nori* nearest to you, roll up the *nori* and rice into a tube with the tuna in the middle. Use the mat as a guide – do not roll it into the food. Roll the rice tightly so that it sticks together and encloses the filling firmly.

7 Carefully roll the sushi off the mat. Make 11 other rolls in the same way, four for each filling ingredient. Do not use wasabi paste with the cucumber. Use a wet knife to cut each roll into six slices and stand them on a platter. Wipe and re-rinse the knife occasionally between cuts to stop the rice sticking. Garnish with *gari* and serve soy sauce with the sushi.

# MISO SOUP

**T**his soup is one of the most commonly eaten dishes in Japan, and it is usually served with every meal. Every family has its unique recipe for this soup, with individual combinations.

### INGREDIENTS

*150g/5oz Japanese silken tofu,*
*10 x 5 x 3cm/4 x 2 x 1¹/₄ in*
*800ml/1¹/₃ pints/3¹/₂ cups kombu and*
*bonito stock or instant dashi*
*10g/¹/₄oz dried wakame seaweed*
*60ml/4 tbsp white or red miso paste*
*2 spring onions, chopped,*
*to garnish*

*SERVES 4*

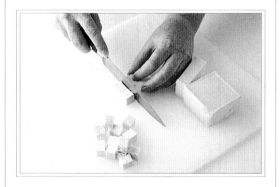

1 Cut the tofu into 1cm/½in cubes. Bring the stock to the boil and reduce the heat.

2 Add the wakame seaweed and simmer for 1–2 minutes.

3 Pour some soup into a bowl and add the miso paste, stirring until it dissolves, and then pour the mixture back into the pan.

4 Add the tofu and heat through for about 1 minute, then serve immediately, while still very hot. Garnish with the chopped spring onions.

### COOK'S TIP
Reduce the heat when the stock boils as it loses flavour if boiled for too long. Similarly, cook the soup long enough to heat the ingredients.

# SHIITAKE MUSHROOM AND EGG SOUP

O *sumashi* means clear soup. This recipe goes particularly well with any sushi, as its delicate flavour complements rather than overpowers the flavour of the fish.

### INGREDIENTS
*600ml/1 pint/2¹/₂ cups kombu and bonito stock or instant dashi*
*4 shiitake mushrooms, stems removed, thinly sliced*
*5ml/1 tsp salt*
*10ml/2 tsp* usukuchi *soy sauce*
*5ml/1 tsp sake or dry white wine*
*2 size 4 eggs*
*¹/₂ punnet of cress, to garnish*

*SERVES 4*

---

### COOK'S TIP
Shiitake mushrooms can be used to make a delicious stock. Just use the water that you have used to soak them in if they are dried.

---

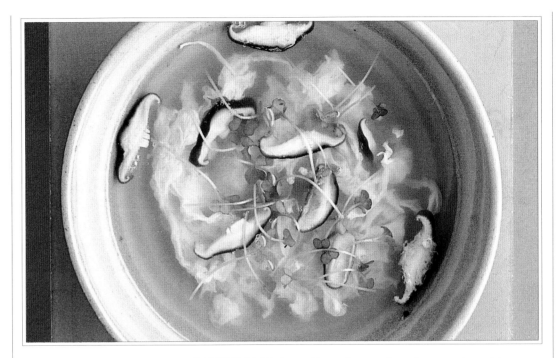

1 Bring the stock to the boil, add the shiitake mushrooms and simmer for about 1–2 minutes. Do not overcook.

2 Add the salt, *usukuchi* soy sauce and sake or wine. Then break the eggs into a bowl and stir well with chopsticks.

3 Pour the egg into the soup in a thin steady stream, in a circular motion – rather like drawing a spiral shape in the soup. To keep the soup clear, the heat must be high enough to set the egg as soon as it is added.

4 Simmer the soup for a few seconds until the eggs are cooked through. Use a pair of chopsticks to break up the egg in order to serve it equally among four bowls. Remove from the heat. Sprinkle with some cress and serve immediately.

# MIXED VEGETABLE SOUP

he main ingredient for this soup is crushed tofu, which is both nutritious and satisfying.

### INGREDIENTS
*150g/5oz fresh Japanese tofu*
*2 dried shiitake mushrooms*
*50g/2oz gobo*
*5ml/1 tsp rice vinegar*
*$^1/_2$ black or white konnyaku, 125g/4$^1/_4$oz*
*30ml/2 tbsp sesame oil*
*115g/4oz mooli, thinly sliced*
*50g/2oz carrot, thinly sliced*
*700ml/generous 1 pint/scant 3 cups kombu and bonito stock or instant dashi*
*pinch of salt*
*30ml/2 tbsp sake or dry white wine*
*7.5ml/1$^1/_2$ tsp mirin*
*45ml/3 tbsp white or red miso paste*
*dash of soy sauce*
*6 mangetouts, trimmed, boiled and thinly sliced, to garnish*

*SERVES 4*

1 Crush the tofu by hand until it resembles a lumpy scrambled egg texture – do not crush it too finely.

2 Wrap the tofu in a dish cloth and put it in a strainer, then pour over plenty of boiling water. Leave the tofu to drain thoroughly for 10 minutes.

3 Soak the dried shiitake mushrooms in tepid water for 20 minutes, then drain them, reserving the soaking water for stock. Remove their stems, and cut the caps into four to six pieces.

4 Use a vegetable brush to scrub the skin off the gobo and slice it carefully into thin shavings. Soak the shavings for about 5 minutes in plenty of cold water with the vinegar added to remove any bitter taste. Drain well.

5 Put the konnyaku in a small saucepan and pour over just enough water to cover it. Bring to the boil over a moderate heat, then drain and allow to cool. Using your hands, tear the konnyaku into 2cm/$^3/_4$in lumps. Do not use a knife as smooth cuts will prevent it from absorbing flavour.

6 Heat the sesame oil in a deep saucepan. Add all the shiitake mushrooms, gobo, mooli, carrot and konnyaku. Stir-fry for 1 minute, then add the tofu and stir well.

7 Pour in the stock and add the salt, sake or wine and mirin. Bring to the boil. Skim the broth and simmer for 5 minutes.

8 In a small bowl, dissolve the miso paste in a little of the soup, then return it to the pan. Simmer the soup for 10 minutes, until the vegetables are soft. Add the soy sauce, then remove from the heat. Serve immediately in four bowls, garnished with the mangetouts.

### COOK'S TIP
Konnyaku is a special cake made from flour that is produced from a root vegetable called devil's tongue. It has a subtle slightly fishy flavour.

# PRAWN AND EGG-KNOT SOUP

There are no set main courses in Japan and all dishes are eaten together. Soup is also eaten for breakfast, when it is typically served with seaweed and a soft-boiled egg.

## INGREDIENTS
*800ml/1¹/₃ pints/3¹/₂ cups kombu and*
*bonito stock or instant dashi*
*5ml/1 tsp* usukuchi *soy sauce*
*salt*
*1 spring onion, thinly sliced,*
*to garnish*

### FOR THE PRAWN SHINJO BALLS
*200g/7oz raw large prawns, shelled,*
*thawed if frozen*
*65g/2¹/₂oz cod fillet, skinned*
*5ml/1 tsp egg white*
*5ml/1 tsp sake or dry white wine, plus an*
*extra dash*
*22.5ml/4¹/₂ tsp cornflour or potato starch*
*2–3 drops soy sauce*

### FOR THE OMELETTE
*1 egg, beaten*
*dash of mirin*
*oil, for cooking*

*SERVES 4*

1 Remove the black vein running down the back of the prawns. Process the prawns, cod, egg white, the sake or wine, cornflour or potato starch, soy sauce and a pinch of salt together in a food processor or blender to make a sticky paste. Alternatively, finely chop the prawns and cod, crush them with the knife's blade and then pound them well in a mortar with a pestle, adding the remaining ingredients.

2 Shape the mixture into four balls and steam for 10 minutes over a high heat. Soak the spring onion in cold water for 5 minutes, then drain.

3 Mix the egg with a pinch of salt and the mirin. Heat a little oil in a frying pan and pour in the egg, tilting the pan to coat it evenly. When the egg has set, turn the omelette over and cook for 30 seconds. Leave to cool.

4 Cut the cooked omelette into long strips, each about 2cm/³/₄in wide. Knot each strip once, place in a strainer and rinse with hot water to remove any excess oil. Bring the stock to the boil and add the *usukuchi* soy sauce, a pinch of salt and a dash of sake or wine.

5 Divide the prawn balls and the egg knots among four serving bowls. Pour in the soup, sprinkle with the spring onion and serve immediately.

# RICE CAKES WITH STRAWBERRIES

**W**hereas traditionally an ingredient such as aduki bean paste would have been the sole accompaniment for these rice cakes, in this fairly modern dessert, fresh fruit is also served.

INGREDIENTS

*100g/3³/₄ oz/scant ¹/₂ cup shiratama-ko powder (rice flour)*
*15ml/1 tbsp sugar*
*cornflour, for dusting*
*10 strawberries*
*115g/4oz/scant ¹/₂ cup canned* neri-an *(Japanese soft aduki bean paste), cut into 5 pieces*

MAKES 5

1 In a microwave-proof bowl, mix the shiratama-ko powder and sugar. Gradually add 200ml/7fl oz/scant 1 cup water. Knead well to make a thick paste.

2 Cover and cook in a microwave (600 or 500W) for 1¹/₂–2 minutes. Alternatively, steam it in a heatproof bowl over a pan of simmering water for 10–15 minutes.

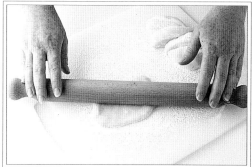

3 Lightly dust a chopping board with a layer of cornflour. Turn out the heated mixture on to it and divide it into five even-size pieces. Using a rolling pin, gently roll out a portion of the mixture into a small oval shape.

4 Put a strawberry and a piece of *neri-an* in the middle. Fold the rice cake in half and serve decorated with a strawberry. Make a further four rice cakes. Eat the rice cakes on the day they are prepared – if left for any longer, they will harden.

# SWEET POTATO, APPLE AND BEAN PASTE CAKES

**A** mixture of mashed sweet potato and a hint of apple is shaped into cubes, covered in batter and then seared in a hot pan to seal in the natural moisture. Aduki bean paste is also made into cakes by the same method.

### INGREDIENTS
*250g/9oz canned* neri-an *(Japanese soft aduki bean paste), divided into 3 pieces*

### FOR THE BATTER
*90ml/6 tbsp plain flour*
*pinch of sugar*
*75ml/5 tbsp water*

### FOR THE STUFFING
*150g/5oz sweet potato, peeled*
*¼ red eating apple, cored and peeled*
*200ml/7fl oz/scant 1 cup water*
*50g/2oz/¼ cup sugar*
*juice of ¼ lemon*

### SERVES 3 (MAKES 6)

1 Put all the ingredients for the batter in a bowl and mix well until smooth. Pour the batter into a large, shallow dish.

2 Dice the sweet potato and soak it in plenty of cold water for 5 minutes to remove any bitterness, then drain well.

3 Coarsely chop the apple and place in a saucepan. Add the water and sweet potato. Sprinkle in 7.5ml/1½ tsp sugar and cook over a moderate heat until the apple and potato are softened.

4 Add the lemon juice and remove the saucepan from the heat. Then drain the sweet potato and apple and crush them to a coarse paste in a mixing bowl with the remaining sugar.

5 Using your hands, shape the mixture into three cubes.

6 Heat a non-stick frying pan. Carefully coat a cube of stuffing mixture in batter, then, taking great care not to burn your fingers, sear each side of the cube on the hot frying pan until the batter has set and cooked through.

7 Repeat this procedure with the remaining stuffing mixture and with the *neri-an*, shaped into similar-size cubes. Arrange on small plates and serve hot or cold.

# GREEN AND YELLOW LAYERED CAKES

**T**his colourful two-tone dessert is made by squeezing contrasting mixtures in a small pouch of muslin or thin cotton. The Japanese title, *Chakin-shibori,* is derived from the preparation technique in which *chakin* means a pouch shape and *shibori* means a moulding action.

### INGREDIENTS
#### FOR THE YOLK MIXTURE (*KIMI-AN*)
*6 size 2 eggs*
*50g/2oz/¼ cup granulated sugar*

#### FOR THE PEA MIXTURE (*ENDO-AN*)
*200g/7oz/1¾ cups fresh peas, shelled*
*40g/11½oz/8 tsp sugar*

*MAKES 6*

1 To make the yolk mixture, hard-boil the eggs. Remove the yolks and sieve them into a bowl. Press the yolk with a spatula, add the sugar and mix well.

2 To make the pea mixture, boil the peas for about 15 minutes, or until they are softened. Drain and place in a mortar, then crush the peas with a pestle and transfer them to a saucepan.

3 Add the sugar and cook, stirring continuously, until the paste is thick. Keep the mixture simmering but ensure that it does not scorch on the bottom of the pan.

4 Spread out the paste in a large dish to cool it down quickly. To maintain its green colour, it is important to cool the paste as quickly as possible.

5 Divide each of the mixtures into six portions. Wet a piece of muslin or thin cotton and wring it out well.

6 Place a lump of pea mixture on the cloth and put a lump of the yolk mixture on top. Wrap it up and squeeze the top of the cloth to mark a spiral pattern on the top of the cakes. Squeezing the cloth also joins the two stuffings together. Make another five cakes in the same way. Serve cold.

# GREEN TEA CAKE

**B**aking cakes for desserts takes on a new twist when using Japanese ingredients. For example, glacé aduki beans *(ama-natto)* are used in the same way as marrons glacés, and the cake remains moist and light.

### INGREDIENTS
*115g/4oz/1 cup plain flour*
*15g/¹/₂oz green tea powder*
*2.5ml/¹/₂ tsp baking powder*
*3 size 3 eggs*
*75g/3oz/¹/₃ cup granulated sugar*
*75g/3oz/¹/₃ cup ama-natto (glacé Japanese aduki beans)*
*65g/2¹/₂oz/5 tbsp lightly salted butter, melted*
*whipped cream, to serve (optional)*

*MAKES AN 18 x 7.5 x 10CM/ 7 x 3 x 4IN CAKE*

1 Preheat the oven to 180°C/350°F/Gas 4. Line and grease a loaf tin. Sift the flour, green tea powder and baking powder together and set aside.

2 In a large heatproof bowl, whisk the eggs and sugar over a saucepan of hot water until pale and thick.

3 Sprinkle the sifted flour over the mixture. Before the flour sinks into the mixture, add the glacé Japanese aduki beans, then fold in the ingredients gently using a spatula. Fold the mixture over from the bottom once or twice. Do not mix too hard. Fold in the melted butter.

4 Pour the mixture into the prepared tin and smooth over the top. Bake the cake in the lower part of the oven for about 35–40 minutes, or until a warm metal skewer inserted into the centre of the cake comes out free of sticky mixture.

5 Turn out the cake on to a wire rack and remove the lining paper while it is hot. Leave to cool. Slice and serve with whipped cream, if liked.

# Basic Recipes

## Boiled Rice

Washing rice is very important as this improves the flavour of the cooked rice. In some recipes, part of the measured quantity of water is replaced with some flavouring.

*480g/1lb 1oz/2¹/₄ cups Japanese rice*
*600ml/1 pint/2¹/₂ cups water*

*Serves 4–6*

1 Wash the rice extremely well, in about six changes of water, and leave to drain through a fine strainer for 30–60 minutes.

2 Transfer the rice to a rice cooker, add the measured water and switch on. Alternatively, use a deep saucepan, cover and cook over a moderate heat until steam comes out. Reduce the heat and simmer for 10–12 minutes. Do not open the saucepan during the cooking process. Finally, before removing the lid, cook the rice over a high heat for 5 seconds.

3 When the rice is cooked, leave it to stand for 15 minutes, then remove the lid and stir the rice once with a wet spatula to remove excess vapour (use a wet spatula in order to prevent the rice from sticking to it). Serve immediately.

## Instant Stock

For speed or convenience when you need a small amount of stock, granules are very good. They are very popular in Japan, and you can find many varieties in Japanese supermarkets. For example, *Hondashi* are kombu seaweed and bonito flake stock granules; *Iriko-dashi* are *Niboshi* or *Iriko* stock granules; concentrated kombu seaweed and bonito flake stock is available in liquid form. There is also a tea bag style instant stock. These are all useful for miso soup and everyday cooking. Follow the packet instructions to use.

## Kombu Seaweed and Bonito Flake Stock

This stock, known as *Ichiban-dashi* is used for delicately flavoured dishes.

*10g/¹/₄ oz dried kombu seaweed,*
*10 x 15cm/4 x 6in*
*10–15g/¹/₄–¹/₂ oz bonito flakes*

*Makes about 800ml/3¹/₃ pints/*
*3¹/₂ cups*

1 Wipe the kombu seaweed with a damp cloth and cut two slits in it with scissors, so that it flavours the stock effectively.

2 Soak it in 900ml/1¹/₂ pints/3³/₄ cups cold water for 30–60 minutes.

3 Heat the kombu in its soaking water over a moderate heat. Just before the water boils, remove the seaweed, otherwise the stock will be dulled. Add the bonito flakes and bring to the boil over a high heat, then remove the pan from the heat.

4 Leave the stock until all the bonito flakes have sunk to the bottom of the pan. Line a strainer with kitchen paper or muslin and place it over a large mixing bowl, then gently strain the stock.

# INDEX

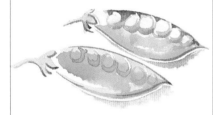